M000251494

DEC 0 3 1996

Hispanic Heritage: Volume 4

Wars of Independence

Richard Sanchez

Published by Abdo & Daughters, 4940 Viking Drive, Suite 622, Edina, MN 55435.

Library bound edition distributed by Rockbottom Books, Pentagon Tower, P.O. Box 36036, Minneapolis, Minnesota 55435.

Photos by:
Bettmann Archive: 7, 9-11, 14-17, 21, 23, 25-26
Archive Photos: 8, 22

Edited by John Hamilton

Library of Congress Cataloging–in–Publication Data
Sanchez, Richard, 1954-
    Wars of independence / Richard Sanchez.
        p.   cm. — (Hispanic heritage ; v. 4)
    Includes bibliographical references and index.
    ISBN 1-56239-334-0. — ISBN 1-56239-384-7 (pbk.)
    1. Latin America—Relations—United States—Juvenile literature. 2. United States—Relations—Latin America—Juvenile literature. 3. Latin America—History—Wars of Independence, 1806–1830—Juvenile literature. 4. Mexican War, 1846–1848—Juvenile literature. 5. United States—History—Civil War, 1861–1865—Participation, Hispanic Americans—Juvenile literature. 6. Spanish-American War, 1898—Juvenile literature. 7. Revolutionaries—Latin America—History—19th century—Juvenile literature. 8. Hispanic Americans—History—19th century—Juvenile literature. [1. Latin America—Relations—United States. 2. United States—Relations—Latin America. 3. Latin America—History—Wars of Independence, 1806–1830. 4. United States—History—Civil War, 1861–1865—Participation, Hispanic American.]   I. Title.   II. Series: Hispanic heritage (Edina, Minn.) ; v. 4.
F1418.S2495   1994
980'.02—dc20   94-33364
                                                                        CIP
                                                                        AC

CONTENTS

1
INTRODUCTION

The United States was still a very young nation at the dawning of the 19th Century. Even so, the world greatly admired this amazing new country. Here there was freedom for people to do great things with their lives and to find happiness. These freedoms were guaranteed rights of every citizen.

No other nation in the world had as its goal freedom for all. And nowhere else was the power to choose leaders placed in the hands of ordinary people. For up until that time, people in countries all around the world were treated as possessions that belonged to kings and queens and emperors and empresses. People were told by government officials where to live and work, what to read and even what to think. They were not allowed to speak out against the wrongs of their leaders. Innocent people could have their homes taken away if the rulers wanted property for their own use. And people could be thrown in jail for the least little thing or be kept from ever receiving a fair trial.

It was so different in the United States. Soon, people from many places around the world began demanding for themselves the same freedoms enjoyed by the citizens of the United States. Nowhere did this desire for liberty burn hotter than in the colonies and provinces of Spain and Portugal during the 1800s.

2
LATIN AMERICAN LIBERATION

The Hispanics who lived in the Spanish and Portuguese colonies were a new people. Their ancestors from Europe had married tribal natives. So the children and grandchildren of these marriages were only part European. Not only that but these Hispanics had been living in the New World for so many years that few thought of Spain or Portugal as their homeland anymore. Europe was just some unknown faraway place to them.

In the Spanish colonies taxes were very high and difficult to pay. The settlers were not allowed to produce the same things grown or made in Spain. Whatever they were permitted to grow or make had to be sold to Spain only and at unfairly low prices.

These laws made the Hispanics in the New World very unhappy. They were ready in the early 1800s to throw off Spanish rule.

THE FIRST FIGHTERS FOR FREEDOM

One of the first liberators of Latin America was Francisco de Miranda. He was born in Caracas, Venezuela, in 1756. Miranda was a hero in the United States for his part in defeating the British at Pensacola, Florida, during the Revolutionary War. Miranda studied the Constitution of the new United

States and wanted to bring the same kind of freedom to Venezuela. In 1805, Miranda left New York by boat with a small army of soldiers determined to end Spanish rule in northern South America. His attempt to start a revolution failed. Six years later, Miranda felt the time was right to try again. He convinced the leaders of Venezuela to declare independence. But many Venezuelans were not ready for freedom. They fought back and defeated Miranda. The year was 1812. Venezuela again became a Spanish possession. Miranda was thrown in prison where he died in 1816.

SIMON BOLIVAR, THE GREAT LIBERATOR

Venezuela did not remain in the hands of Spain for very long. An even greater liberator by the name of Simon Bolivar had come along. Bolivar was born in Venezuela in 1783. He was a friend of Miranda and had also lived for a time in the United States. Bolivar shared Miranda's dream of seeing Spain driven from Venezuela as well as neighboring Columbia. In 1814, Bolivar led an army against Bogota, the capital city of Columbia. The fighting was fierce. Eventually, Bogota and all of Columbia fell to Bolivar. He set up a new government and proclaimed Columbia free. But Spain launched a counterattack against Bolivar and took back Columbia in 1816. Bolivar escaped capture and went into hiding for two years.

Bolivar rebuilt his army and this time attacked a few important cities in Venezuela before crossing over the Andes Mountains to fight the Spanish in Peru and Ecuador. Bolivar's army was outnum-

Francisco Miranda (facing page), from Venezuela. Miranda was one of the first Latin American revolutionists.

6

Simon Bolivar helped put an end to Spanish rule in northern South America.

bered but he was a very wise and crafty general. Bolivar always managed to trick the Spanish and stay one step ahead of them. Finally, he outfoxed Spain at the Battle of Boyaca in August, 1819. From then on, Bolivar and his troops could not be stopped. In 1821, Bolivar attacked once more in Venezuela and won. Spanish rule in northern South America came to an end in 1821. That same year, Venezuela, Columbia, Ecuador and Panama formed a single nation known as the Republic of Columbia. Bolivar was chosen to be its first president.

Spain continued to control the remainder of South America. In 1823, Bolivar's army brought freedom to Peru. From some of the liberated lands in the Andes a new country was formed. It was named Bolivia in honor of Simon Bolivar.

These were times of great joy for the people. But only a few years later the people began fighting among themselves. In 1830, the republic broke apart. Bolivar was heartbroken and soon died of poor health.

Other Heroes
Of Freedom

Another great liberator who fought alongside Bolivar was Bernardo O'Higgins. O'Higgins freed Chile. He became Chile's leader. He tried to do the right things. But he ruled the country like he alone owned it. The people soon tired of O'Higgins bossing them around. They rebelled and forced him to flee the country.

Argentina was set free by Jose de San Martin. San Martin was born in Buenos Aires, Argentina, in 1778. The people turned against their liberator when he tried to set up a constitutional monarchy like in England.

Brazil won its independence from Portugal in 1822. War erupted between Brazil and Argentina in 1825 over control of the province of Uruguay. Neither side could muster a victory and so Uruguay went free on its own.

Above: *Bernardo O'Higgins, liberator of Chile.*
Below: *Argentina's Jose de San Martin.*

3
REVOLUTION IN MEXICO

Revolution came to Mexico in the dark of night on September 16, 1810. A priest by the name of Miguel Hidalgo started it all by breaking into the jail in the town of Dolores and freeing the people who had been wrongly put behind bars. Father Hidalgo and the escaped prisoners ran to the church of Dolores. They began ringing the steeple bell. The people of Dolores were awakened by the battlecry that is now famous: "Long live independence! Long live America! Death to bad government!"

The Spanish army was taken

Miguel Hidalgo.

by surprise at first by Father Hidalgo and his rapidly growing ranks of followers. The Spanish troops lost several battles. But then they started gaining the upper hand. Soon, it was the revolutionaries and Father Hidalgo who were tasting defeat. Father Hidalgo was captured and executed in 1811.

The freedom fighters continued to wage war against the Spanish. By 1821, the Spanish were worn down from the uprisings all across Latin America. Spain had had enough. Mexico was granted independence that same year.

Many struggles for power followed. The strongest leader to arise was Antonio Lopez de Santa Anna. Santa Anna was a clever general. He actually fought against Mexico on the side of Spain during the revolution. But he switched sides after Mexico won. In 1829, Spain decided it wanted back Mexico.

Mexican General Antonio Lopez de Santa Anna.

War broke out. This time, Santa Anna fought to save Mexico. The Spanish were defeated and Santa Anna was hailed as the hero of Mexico. He became president of the country in 1833. But Santa Anna turned out to be a cruel dictator.

In 1821, neighboring Guatemala, El Salvador, Honduras and Nicaragua also declared themselves free from Spain. The four former colonies then became partners with Mexico in a union of Central American countries. But this union began falling apart in 1838 and the five countries went their separate ways.

4
FREEDOM FOR
THE ISLANDS

The Caribbean island of Puerto Rico was a haven for revolutionaries from other Spanish colonies who needed a place to hide out. Yet Puerto Ricans wanted freedom from Spain for themselves.

Ramon Power Giralt was a Puerto Rican liberator who fought for independence by working within the Spanish system of government. He went to Spain to represent the interests of Puerto Rico. In 1812 Power convinced the Spanish rulers to give Puerto Rico a limited constitution that guaranteed basic rights of the people to vote, to speak out against wrongs, to receive a fair trial, and to enjoy the use of any land they might own. But later, a new government came to power in Spain and ended many of Puerto Rico's constitutional freedoms.

The first awakening of desire for independence in the Philippine Islands of the Pacific Ocean began around 1834. That was the year Spain began allowing ships from other countries to dock in the islands' harbors. The Philippine economy grew. People suddenly had money to afford the nicer things in life. Many of the newly wealthy sent their children to special schools in the United States. There, the children learned about America's freedoms. The children returned home to the Philippines eager for the bell of liberty to begin ringing throughout the islands as well.

5
THE ROLE OF THE UNITED STATES

The United States was only a little interested in what was going on in Latin America during the first few years of the 19th Century. The country had other things to think about in those days. Things like another war with the British in 1812.

But by the 1820s, the United States began feeling more should be done to help Latin America become free. President James Monroe in 1823 declared the Western Hemisphere off-limits to the nations of Europe. He said the people of Latin America should be free to rule themselves. His declaration became known as the Monroe Doctrine. But the United States did not yet have enough military might to back up Monroe's words. In Spain, the Monroe Doctrine was laughed at and ignored. The Spanish knew the United States could do little to stop them from doing what they wanted in Latin America.

Attitudes in the United States began to change just a few years after the Monroe Doctrine. Many people and leaders came to believe in a different doctrine called "manifest destiny." Those who believed in manifest destiny felt that God wanted the United States to take over all the lands of North America, from sea to shining sea. The doctrine of "manifest destiny" gave the United States reason to push west across the frontier wilderness and provinces of Mexico during the middle and late 1800s.

6
THE CALIFORNIA EXPERIENCE

One of the first acts of newly freed Mexico in 1821 was to take away all the farm lands owned by the Franciscan priests who had built missions throughout California. The lands were then given to native-born Hispanic families. Some of the lands were used for cattle ranching, while the rest continued to be used for farming.

Much money could be made in cattle ranching. The people who owned the ranches became so wealthy that life in California from the 1820s to the 1840s seemed like one great big party after another.

The first signs that the merry times might soon end came in 1836. That year, citizens of California demanded that Mexico show more concern for them. There were worries about invasion from Europe, but the Mexican government didn't seem to care that the people felt unsafe. So the

California cowboys branding cattle.

An early Californian flag, with symbols of the star and bear.

people asked Mexico to allow them to set up a state government to handle problems within California. Mexico agreed to let them do it. But Mexico insisted on picking the governor. The person who was chosen governor did not please the commander of California's army. General Mariano Guadalupe Vallejo instead wanted his nephew Juan Batista Alvardo to be governor. Vallejo led a rebellion and saw to it that Alvarado was placed in office.

Then, real trouble began brewing. From out of the east by wagon train came Anglo settlers. Hordes of them. General Vallejo bid them welcome. He wanted even more of them to come. He thought they would be good for the state by helping build its economy. But his nephew Governor Alvarado wanted all of them to go away. He worried that the newcomers would try to take over. And that's just what they did. In 1846, the Anglos demanded California be given to them. They even made a flag for themselves that pictured a bear beneath a single star. The Hispanic leaders refused to do what the Anglos wanted. The Anglos rose up in rebellion. Their uprising became known as the Bear Flag Revolt. This brought soldiers from the United States marching into California. The soldiers helped the Anglo settlers end Hispanic control by 1848.

7

THE SOUTHWEST TAKEN AWAY

California was one of the last places Anglo pioneers settled. Texas was one of the first.

As early as 1803, the United States claimed to own much of what today is Texas. But Spain disagreed. Spain said it was the rightful owner. The dispute over Texas continued for 15 years. Finally, in 1819, the United States gave up and agreed the land was Spain's.

An Anglo by the name of Moses Austin asked Mexico for permission to start a colony in Texas. Austin died a short time later. But Mexico gave the OK for his son Stephen Austin to come into Texas. Austin's colony began in 1821. It grew. Before long, the Anglo population in Texas had multiplied into the tens of thousands and their settlements had spread far and wide. This greatly worried Mexico. It was decided that no more Anglos should be allowed into Texas. The Anglos did not like being told they were unwelcome. They also did not like the new laws Mexico had made so that life for the Anglos would become much more difficult. The Anglos grew so angry that they started a rebellion.

In 1835, Mexico's General Santa Anna led an army against the rebel Anglo settlers. Many of the settlers were killed. The battle best remembered was The Alamo in San Antonio. A small band of Anglos had barricaded themselves inside a mission chapel called The Alamo and for nearly two weeks held back Santa Anna's troops. All the defenders of The Alamo were killed. But that didn't stop the Anglos in 1836 from declaring Texas independent of Mexico.

The Anglos fought with all their might. They fought so hard that they eventually captured Santa Anna himself.

The war with Mexico never really came to an end. It just sort of quieted down to where it was barely noticed. But things heated up once again in 1841 when the Anglos tried without success to invade New Mexico.

The fight for the Alamo.

In 1845, the Anglos decided to make Texas part of the United States. The next year, the Mexican army swooped down on the Anglos in a final attempt at forcing them out of Texas. But this time Mexico wasn't fighting poorly armed pioneers. It was the well-equipped military of the United States.

8
MEXICO AND THE UNITED STATES GO TO WAR

A full-scale war between Mexico and the United States had broken out because both nations wanted Texas. The year was 1846. The war lasted until 1848.

Gradually the army of Mexico was beaten back. The United States troops fought their way south into Mexico. The war ended when the United States captured Mexico City.

A peace treaty was then signed. It became known as the Treaty of Guadalupe Hidalgo. Mexico agreed to give up its claim to Texas. Mexico also agreed to sell to the United States the lands of California, Arizona, New Mexico, Colorado and Kansas. The treaty also promised full United States citizenship to all the people living in those places.

The treaty promised one other important thing. Hispanics could keep whatever lands they owned before the war.

Many Hispanics took great comfort in that promise. But they were soon to discover that the United States was unwilling to stand by its word. Much of the land that Hispanics had been told was theirs to possess soon was stolen from them. Why? Because certain Anglos planned to build railroads and cities on those lands. The land was valuable for those purposes. But the railroad owners and city developers did not want to pay for it. How was the land stolen? The people who wanted the land used trickery and threats to make Hispanics give up their ownership rights.

Of course, not all of the land was stolen. Some Anglos did the honorable thing and paid a handsome price for what they wanted. And not all Hispanics had their lands taken. Some continued to own them without any problems.

Some Hispanics whose lands were stolen tried to fight back. One such person was Tibirico Vasquez. He became known as the Robin Hood of his time. In the 1870s, Vasquez and several other outlaws joined together to terrorize the land thieves. Vasquez was famous for robbing stagecoaches carrying wealthy people and then giving the money to the poor. Sheriff's posses were sent out on horseback to try and capture Vasquez. He escaped many times. Then, in May, 1874, a posse caught him near Los Angeles. He was found guilty of his crimes and was hanged to death less than a year later.

Other Hispanics without land wandered about the Southwest in search of jobs and new homes. Many found they were welcomed in Tucson, Arizona. Beginning in the 1860s, Hispanics helped transform dusty little Tucson into a prosperous big city. The mayor of Tucson was a man named Estevan Ochoa. Ochoa saw to it that an excellent public school system was created for Hispanics in Tucson. But Ochoa made every student learn English. He believed the only way Hispanics could compete in business against Anglos was to be able to read, write and speak their language.

9
THE CIVIL WAR

There came a time that the United States went to war against itself. It happened in the year 1861. It was called back then the War Between the States. Today it is simply known as the Civil War.

The Civil War was fought to bring freedom to people who were forced to live as slaves. There were many citizens in the southern part of the country who believed it was OK to own slaves. The slaves had come from Africa and were made to work without pay on farms or as servants in homes.

Other Americans living mostly in the northern part of the United States believed it was wrong for one human to be the owner of somebody else. They tried for many long years to get a law that would end slavery. Their attempts were blocked every time by those people who favored slavery.

At last it looked as if a law against slavery might be coming. Abraham Lincoln was elected as President and he had vowed to end slavery. The slave owners were so upset that they decided to start their own country. This new country was called the Confederate States of America and it was made up entirely of states from the South.

Fighting began after the Confederates fired cannons at a fort belonging to the United States in Charleston, South Carolina. Many lives were lost during the four years of the Civil War. Some of its greatest heroes were Hispanics.

Hispanic units of the United States Army in New Mexico helped knock out Confederate forces from Texas at the Battle of Valverde. This one battle was among the most horrifying of any fought during the Civil War. It also was as far west as the fighting ever reached. The battle began after the South invaded New Mexico. The Hispanic defenders knew they were going to lose the battle because the attackers had so many more soldiers, guns, horses and cannons. But that did not stop the Hispanic troops from fighting with all their strength and courage. In the end, the Texas troops won. But they lost so many men that Texas was never able to win any other big battles for the rest of the war.

Perhaps the most famous Hispanic hero of the Civil War was Admiral David Glasgow Farragut. Farragut was born near Knoxville, Tennessee in 1801. His father was a Navy hero of the Revolutionary War. The stories of bravery and self-sacrifice Farragut heard his father tell about the war for independence led him to join the Navy himself as soon as he was old enough. Years later the Civil War started. President Lincoln knew Farragut was one of the best and brightest military men in the country. So he asked Farragut to lead a Navy attack against the city of New Orleans. Farragut spent a long time carefully planning the attack. It took place April 18, 1862. On the west bank of the Mississippi at the entrance to New Orleans stood a much-feared fortress. Farragut's ships opened fired on the fortress with their cannons. The cannons

Admiral David Glasgow Farragut, famous Hispanic hero of the Civil War.

in the fortress fired back. Bombs exploded everywhere. Thick, black smoke filled the air over the water as well as over the land. It went on like this for days. Many of the men on Farragut's ships were killed and some of the boats were sunk. Finally, at dawn on April 24, Farragut led 17 ships in a run straight past the fortress. They sailed into New Orleans and captured the city. President Lincoln rewarded Farragut by making him the highest-ranking admiral in the entire Navy.

Farragut then continued north up the river and captured Memphis, Tennessee. The fleet kept going and captured the cities of Vicksburg, Galveston and Corpus Christi. By the end of 1862, the Union Navy held all of the Gulf Coast except for Mobile Bay.

Mobile Bay was the most dangerous battle of all because the South had protected their forts there with launchers that could fire torpedoes at attacking ships. When Farragut's fleet began its attack, the ship that led the way was hit by a torpedo. It sunk. The captain of the ship following behind the one that sunk wanted to turn back because the water was criss-crossed with torpedoes. But instead Farragut shouted from the bridge of the third warship, "Damn the torpedoes! Full speed ahead!" The fleet made it through and captured New Orleans.

The capture of New Orleans— the fleet passing forts on the Mississippi.

10
HEADING TOWARD
THE 20TH CENTURY

The Civil War ended in 1865. The South surrendered. The slaves were freed. The Confederate states were welcomed back into a union with the North. After all those years of bloodshed, now it was time for the country to heal.

The years went by and the United States changed from a nation of farms and ranches to a nation of crowded cities and busy factories.

A monument called the Statue of Liberty was built at the entrance of New York harbor and it became a beacon that invited people from all over the world to come and live in the United States. For it was said that in the United States anything was possible for those willing to work hard and play by the rules.

Among the immigrants attracted by the lure of freedom and riches in the United States were Hispanics from Latin America and the Philippines. Unrest and poverty were all too common in their homelands.

The Statue of Liberty in New York City.

11
MORE FIGHTS FOR FREEDOM IN THE HISPANIC WORLD

Many Latin American countries that obtained independence in the early 19th Century were in constant struggles to remain free. Guatemala, El Salvador, Honduras and Nicaragua each fell under the control of powerful dictators. Some of the dictators were actually quite concerned about the welfare of the people they ruled. But most were interested only in enriching themselves, their families and their closest friends at the expense of the people. The fear, violence and tyranny common in Central America lasted long past the close of the century.

Panama tried to break away from Columbia in 1830, 1840 and again in 1850 without success. After that there were 53 different revolts in Panama up until 1903 when independence from Columbia finally was won.

Mexico's General Santa Anna proclaimed himself president forever in 1853. He was toppled from power two years later. In 1864, Mexico was invaded by France. But Mexico under the leadership of President Benito Juarez stopped the French from taking over. Porfirio Diaz ruled Mexico for the last third of the 19th Century. He started as a friend of the people. But then he turned into a hated dictator who lived like a European king while most everyone else lived in poverty.

In the Philippines, a doctor named Jose Rizal launched a political party to set the Philippines free from Spain. But he was arrested and put to death in 1896. That same year there began a secret society called the Katipunan. Members of the Katipunan stirred up the people and started a revolt led by Emilio Aguinaldo.

In Puerto Rico, the cry for freedom rose louder during the 1850s. Spain responded in 1887 by unleashing the Year of Terror in which hundreds of liberty lovers were rounded up and jailed. Many were tortured while others were killed. Finally, at the start of the year 1898, Puerto Rico was given permission by Spain to create a government that gave people their first real taste of independence. It didn't last long. Only a few months later war broke out between Spain and the United States.

In Cuba, the hero who fought hardest against government tyranny was Jose Julian Marti. Marti started young in his crusade to rid Cuba of Spanish control. As a teen-ager he was arrested for criticizing Spain. As an adult he was jailed again for trying to stir up rebellion. Marti moved to the United States and soon was plotting with other Cuban patriots to attack the Spanish army guarding the island. In late 1894, Marti led an invasion of Cuba. But the attack failed. However, less than

Jose Julian Marti, crusader who fought to rid Cuba of Spanish control.

a year later, a revolution broke out from within Cuba. The people proclaimed Marti their supreme chief. But then came the Battle of Dos Rios in 1895. Marti was wounded so badly that he died a short time later. The people were saddened when they heard the news of Marti's death. But by giving his life for his country, Marti inspired the people to fight all the harder to win their freedom.

Above: *The battleship U.S.S. Maine.* Below: *The Maine mysteriously blows up on Feb. 15, 1898 while anchored in the harbor at Havana, Cuba. More than 250 sailors died.*

12
THE SPANISH–AMERICAN WAR

Toward the last remaining years of the 19th Century, America's newspapers began carrying reports of terrible living conditions in Cuba. The newspapers competed to see which publication could publish the day's most heartbreaking story about the Spanish-ruled island. Most readers were shocked by what the papers said. People began writing to Congress to demand Spain give the Cubans their freedom.

The public was so angry that talk of war against Spain was soon heard. However, President William McKinley and many members of Congress wanted peace. Then, on Feb. 15, 1898, the battleship U.S.S. Maine mysteriously blew up while anchored in the harbor at Havana, Cuba. More than 250 sailors died. No one ever found out the cause of the explosion. But, back in America, the newspapers blamed Spain. Now people were so eager for war that there was no turning back.

The United States declared war in April, 1898. The American Navy steamed across the Pacific Ocean to attack the Spanish fleet protecting the Philippines. Nearly all of Spain's ships were sunk during the Battle of Cavite in Manila Bay on May 1, 1898.

In Puerto Rico, United States Navy warships blasted away at the city of San Juan before sending

3,400 soldiers ashore. That happened at the end of July, 1898. Less than three weeks later the fighting was over. Spain surrendered and turned over to the United States the islands of Puerto Rico, Cuba and the Philippines.

13
EPILOGUE

Hispanics born in the United States and Hispanics who were newcomers to the country faced many hardships with the arrival of the 20th Century and modern times. That was the bad news. The good news was that those Hispanics were strong and determined to overcome whatever difficulties came their way. That was the lesson learned in the fight for freedom.

Hispanics in the new era that was then coming showed over and over again the way to achieve greatness. Hispanic success in business, education, science, the arts and politics became legendary in 20th Century America.

GLOSSARY

CONSTITUTION

A set of laws that govern the behavior of a nation.

DICTATOR

A ruler who has total and absolute control over a nation.

IMMIGRANT

A person who comes to live in a country in which he or she was not born.

INDEPENDENCE

To be free of control by a government.

INVASION

An attempt by one group or country to take over another land by armed attack.

LIBERATOR

A person who brings freedom to a land under the control of a government.

PATRIOT

Someone who loves his or her country.

PIONEER

Someone who is the first to settle a new land.

Posse

A group of citizens who search for and attempt to capture a wanted criminal.

Rebellion

The use of force to throw out a government.

Revolution

(See rebellion.)

Taxes

Money demanded from citizens by their government to pay for an army, new roads and many types of services.

Torpedo

A bomb shaped like a rocket that travels through the water on its own power and that explodes when it smashes into an object such as a boat.

Treaty

An agreement between two countries.

Union

The act of two or more things joining together as one.

Uprising

(See rebellion).

BIBLIOGRAPHY

Anderson, Joan. *Spanish Pioneers of the Southwest*, 1989. Lodestar Books/E.P. Dutton, New York.

Bailey, Bernadine. *Famous Latin-American Liberators*, 1960. Vail-Ballou Press, Binghampton, NY.

Tuck, Jay Nelson & Vergara, Norma Coolen. *Heroes of Puerto Rico*, 1969. Fleet Press Corp., NY, NY.

Lepthien, Emilie U. *The Philippines*, 1984, Children's Press, Chicago, IL.

Melzer, Milton. *The Hispanic American*, 1982. Thomas Y Crowell, New York.

Sinnott, Susan. *Extraordinary Hispanic Americans*, 1991. Children's Press, Chicago.

Various contributors. *World Book Encyclopedia*. Field Enterprises, Chicago.

Various contributors. *Encyclopaedia Britannica*. Encyclopaedia Britannica Inc., London and Chicago.

INDEX